IN DEED, INDEED

IN DEED, INDEED
TEACHING AND LEARNING IN A ONE ROOM SCHOOL

Back row, left to right: Gladys Dart, Rebecca Holmberg, Robert Thompson, Carol Lee Blackburn. Front row, left to right: Ralph Holmberg, John Dart, Jean Blackburn, Diane Dart, Jim Dart, Jonathon Blackburn, Shirley Holmberg, Dawn Monroe

GLADYS DART & ALFRED WRIGHT

Outkirts Press, Inc.
Denver, Colorado

The opinions expressed in this manuscript are solely the opinions of the author and do not represent the opinions or thoughts of the publisher. The author has represented and warranted full ownership and/or legal right to publish all the materials in this book.

In Deed, Indeed
Teaching and Learning in a One Room School
All Rights Reserved.
Copyright © 2010 Gladys Dart & Alfred Wright
v5.0

This book may not be reproduced, transmitted, or stored in whole or in part by any means, including graphic, electronic, or mechanical without the express written consent of the publisher except in the case of brief quotations embodied in critical articles and reviews.

Outskirts Press, Inc.
http://www.outskirtspress.com

ISBN: 978-1-4327-3956-0

Outskirts Press and the "OP" logo are trademarks belonging to Outskirts Press, Inc.

PRINTED IN THE UNITED STATES OF AMERICA

Dedicated to our students, our richest resource.

The highest result of education is tolerance.

    Helen Keller, 'Optimism,' 1903
    U.S. blind & deaf educator (1880 – 1968)

Acknowledgements

I wish to acknowledge so many who have encouraged me to record my educational experience, I express my gratitude. It has sustained me inspirationally to finally make it become a reality. Frank Jones receives special accolades for initiating the reestablishment of a one-room school in Manley Hot Springs and giving me the opportunity to make my dreams come true teaching in one.

I give special thanks to Liza Vernet, who enriched the students and my own experience with her creative volunteer work in the classroom. She rescued projects like the Christmas movie when I was ready to discard them. She gifted me with a tape recorder, admonished me, and encouraged me to write my experience or record it in some manner. She persisted in making this project become a reality.

I acknowledge Heidi Wright, who was instrumental in making this written experience become a reality when it became a part of the celebration of the fiftieth anniversary since the reestablishment of the school. I am also grateful for how much she recognizes and appreciates the value of a one-room school education.

Finally, I want to acknowledge the persistent encouragement for the last twenty years by Dr. Rudy Krejci, a retired philosophy professor, who told me that the story of a teacher in a one-room school in a small village in Alaska was worth telling. I hope you think he was right.

Introduction

We must give credit to Joee Ray Redington, who was a middle-elementary student when I became his teacher, for making it easy to title our written effort.

We came in from recess one day. As we were taking off our coats, he came up to me with a big smile on his face.

He said, "That was a good thing that happened out there."

I said, "Indeed."

He replied, "You know I really like the way you say 'Indeed' when something good happens."

Foreword

The year 2008 is a defining moment to recollect fifty years of memories since the establishment of a one-room school in Manley Hot Springs, a small village in Interior Alaska.

With these memories came the realization of the advantages and disadvantages of teaching and learning in that unique environment. The same uniqueness gave the opportunity to capitalize on the challenges that environment creates. The main objective was to translate these challenges to enrich the students' educational experiences.

These experiences are what memories are made of. Through the years, sharing these memories with students, parents, educators, friends, and others, have brought countless hours of pleasant conversation. On occasion, although I had been encouraged to put these memories on permanent record, I did not actively pursue the suggestion. However, I did think it was a good idea.

It became a great idea when Mrs. Heidi Wright, the present principal-teacher, approached me. The students were doing a local history project and it included the school. I consented with gratitude when she asked for my involvement. I was especially motivated when she suggested that one of her students, Alfred Wright, wanted to assist me with the project. It seemed the perfect time to exercise once more my personal belief that we are never too old to learn and never too young to teach.

Alfred's Words

I admit that at first I was reluctant to start this project with Gladys. As a fourteen year-old freshman, being outside of my peer group made me feel uncomfortable. However, after the first few writing sessions I was eager to join Gladys to help her with this project.

I always wanted to know more about the school's history, and this seemed like a good opportunity to expand my knowledge. Working with a person like Gladys is an opportunity that few people my age get. I think it will benefit me greatly, and help me gain an understanding of my past. "You need to know where you were before you know where you are."

Gladys and Alfred working on their book.

Contents

Acknowledgements ix
Introduction xi
Foreword xiii
Defining Values 7
With Respect 13
On Discipline 19
Family Values 25
School Values 33
Country Values 43
Reestablishing Manley Hot Springs School 53
Learning and Teaching in a One-Room School 61
Starting Classroom Traditions 67
Facing the Challenges of Inadequacy 81
Reading 89
Testing 99
Technology 105
Tolerance 115
The Last Word 123

Part 1 - Indeed

I think that somehow, we learn who we really are and then live with that decision.

Eleanor Roosevelt
U.S. diplomat & reformer (1884 - 1962)

Chapter 1
Defining Values

CHAPTER 1

Defining Values

I believe in the adage, "You need to know where you've been to know where you're going", and just as strongly, I believe in the adage, "You are what you were." To the latter adage, I would only add a phrase to say, "You are what you were and who you want to become."

This adage has served me as a guiding light to finding answers and solutions big and small. This adage in time has built a strong foundation to serve as a point of reference to help me express a viewpoint, a standard, or a value that reflects my being.

The values that represent who I am have their roots in three different areas that are institutionally based. I would best define them as family, school, and country. To further define family, I do not limit it to my immediate lineage. Rather, I prefer to think of the family as an extension beyond the home to everyone everywhere that we can embrace as one family. I also define school beyond the formal institutions that we enroll in as students to further our education. I prefer to define school as an institution without walls. We are "schooled" anywhere at anytime in any situation that furthers our education. It becomes an ongoing activity that is part of our daily lives throughout our entire life. *To me it also means that we are never too old to learn, nor too young to teach.*

The third general area that defines my values is country. The gift that everyone in America is given is the opportunity to live in an environment of diversity and the enrichment it brings into our daily lives. We are rewarded with a greater historical understanding. We are rewarded with a greater racial understanding. We are rewarded with a greater cultural understanding.

When I was asked if I could express my values in terms that were not institutional I came to this conclusion. Values are so gestalten they are difficult to delineate. Generally speaking, my family had the greatest impact in molding my moral standards. The school's greatest impact was molding my search for truth. The country's greatest impact was to mold my standard of patriotism. Through the years these values have served as a guiding light in my daily activities inside and outside the classroom.

Alfred's Words

In my experience at the school these values are used in day-to-day life. Gladys and I have talked about these, and she told me that at my age I will not think of my life in values. During this project I have started reflecting on the history of Manley Hot Springs. In our school history project I have learned of Manley Hot Springs during the time before Gladys even arrived.

Chapter 2
With Respect

CHAPTER **2**

With Respect

In retrospect, it amazes me how frequently I have taken the opportunity to remember who and where I came from when I needed to know who I had become and where I wanted to go. Decisions resulting from values learned earlier inevitably would create moments of reminiscence.

Memories are meant to be put to good use. Sometimes memories are like a compass to guide you in the right direction. Sometimes memories are like opening a gift that would be put to wide use. Even better, wisdom gained from them is best when it is shared.

My greatest gift was my family, who, in their daily practice, fostered the spirit of unconditional love and respect of individuality. They demanded acceptance of responsibility, and maintained an unequivocal standard of integrity and trust.

I was the seventh child in a family of thirteen children. My parents, who were married in the first decade of the twentieth century, were proud advocates of Planned Parenthood. During their engagement, in planning their married life, they decided they would have twelve children. Their third child died, unfortunately, in infancy. So we were raised as a family of twelve children.

We were born into an interesting sequence of three older boys, three older girls, three younger boys, and three younger girls. Whether by instinct, or design, or both, my parents used this to their advantage, and ours, in setting behavioral standards and values. Younger children were taught to listen to the older ones with the same respect for authority they acknowledged in our parents and other adults. On the other hand, older children had to earn the respect of the younger ones by becoming role models that met the standards they learned from our parents and other adults.

Over the years, more and more I came to appreciate the model, or models, my parents set as their example. We were not lectured to. Instead, adhering to the

IN DEED INDEED

philosophy that actions speak louder than words, which had a longer and more lasting impact.

These actions defined themselves into two distinct categories. Minor infractions resulted when an action created an unhappy reaction, or if it resulted in creating an unsafe situation or possible injury. In those cases, we were reprimanded with a reminder, in no uncertain terms, that in our home, we not only accepted responsibility ourselves, but we were also responsible for the happiness and safety of others.

My father used to reprimand us with the Finnish phrase "Merkillinen kakara" and the tone of those words was all we needed to hear to stop acting out and change our behavior.

I heard this many times throughout my childhood. When I was high-school age I remember a conversation with an older sister when she said, " I never heard Father swear. Did you?"

I was really surprised. I said, "He used to swear at us a lot."

Then she asked me, "When did he do that?"

I said, "Didn't you remember when he called us a 'Merkillinen kakara' when he scolded us?"

She broke into laughter when she answered, "He wasn't swearing. He was saying 'You remarkable urchin.'"

The profound effect of my childhood experiences helped me formulate my disciplinary techniques in the classroom. In all my years of teaching, there was only one rule to remember, "In our school we will keep our children happy and safe."

Using this as a standard, it was easier to help a child understand between right and wrong. If the student did not understand the difference, it served as concrete reference of what is not acceptable at school, even though the behavior might be acceptable elsewhere. Another important difference when such an occasion for discipline arose was the importance of keeping it on a one-to-one give-and-take basis in addressing the specific infraction. It was easier under those conditions to create a feeling of cooperation rather than confrontation. Finally, it helped to keep it short and simple. It made the lesson easier to remember and reduced the possibilities of misunderstanding.

So an infraction was considered minor if it was a verbal exchange that created an unhappy result, or a physical contact that did not, but had the potential for physical injury or property damage.

An infraction became major when it was knowingly committed. This also meant that the one committing the infraction fully understood that although the behavior might be acceptable at home or elsewhere, it was not acceptable at our school. Punishment usually, but not always, included retribution greater than just an apology or its equivalent.

To the best of my ability and insistence I stressed the importance of truthfulness when discipline was involved. If a wrong had been committed, small or big, they should not be scared to come forth whether anybody was aware of it or not. I also stressed similar situations that have happened and will happen to all of us and full acknowledgement is the first step to a solution and we are there to help each other.

Once, when a student broke a window, playing ball, when school was not in session, he came to my home to tell me. He offered to pay for it before I had a chance to say anything. I accepted the offer, but when school maintenance paid for it, I asked him whether he wanted a refund or give it as a donation to the student fund. When he opted for the student fund I told him it was best we make it anonymous. I did not want the children to thank him for breaking a window. I thanked him with a hug.

Alfred's Words

Gladys's guidelines that Gladys began using are still followed in our school. Now we have a slightly different policy, but the intent remains the same. I have been chastised for doing things here that I would not do at home, and the teachers make it clear right away why what I did was not acceptable at school. I did not know before that Gladys's original views were the ones my teachers practiced in school.

Gladys circa 1970

Chapter 3
On Discipline

CHAPTER **3**

On Discipline

Looking back fifty years, living in an environment with limited transportation and communication access to the outside world made disciplinary and relationship activities easier to establish and maintain. This is the way it was in my family and this is the way it was at school.

When I thought about how time changes, memories went back to my childhood. Comparisons and contrasts came to mind. They both became more obvious as life evolved from a simpler to a more complicated society. They both made more apparent the transparency of how constant and unchanging the values of common courtesy and respect for each other remain. Equally important, the vehicle that enforced those values was the power of sticking to the truth, and communication, communication, communication.

I was born and raised in a large family in a small town. Life felt secure because these values set the parameters, limitations and freedoms were well established. I was able to exercise this background professionally. Teaching in a multi-grade one-room school in a small village had similarities and differences I could relate to.

It is a rare day when a teacher does not have to address infractions of a minor nature. Through the years, the disciplinary actions remained constant on the premise that safety and happiness were the criteria for judgment.

The big change that I became aware of over the years, more so in the recent past, was the change in attitudes and ways people treat each other. This applied to children and adults alike. In the past, when life was simpler, we, as adults, had better control over the behavior we expected from our children and ourselves. Consequently, it was easier to serve as role models.

The advent of new technology, improved telephone communication, television, the internet, and easier access to outside influences has impacted and complicated disciplinary behavior, especially in the areas of language, violence, and self-gratification. We also have been slower to recognize, address, and accept the social and moral responsibilities to keep abreast of these changes. It is the biggest challenge we have to meet in our responsibilities towards our children.

As teachers, we have been professionally trained to fulfill our duty to make certain that we stay up-to-date in our understanding of present policy, rules and regulations, and state and federal laws. Our training has prepared us to evaluate and make necessary changes when the occasion or need arises.

Teaching in a one-room school in a small village was a constant learning experience for me as well. In my family there was no tolerance or excuse for rude behavior. The main concern was the effect rudeness had on the victim. The first offense was a reprimand. If it occurred again the freedom to participate with the rest of the family was lost until "We had learned our lesson."

As a teacher, the lesson I learned was one I appreciated more as the years went by. The lesson I learned was the fallacy we hear all too often in the saying " Sticks and stones may break my bones, but words will never hurt me." Words do hurt us. Sticks and stones hurt us, and we do not hesitate to do everything possible to aid in the healing process. Scars whether physical or emotional are sad reminders of these experiences.

In fact words hurt just as deeply, or more. We are not always as aware or as sensitive and urgent in promoting the healing process. The scars that could serve as reminders are more difficult to see and too much of the time, we do not look for symptoms that need attention. In my experience as a teacher, I would not tolerate students calling each other stupid. Many years later, after I retired I was told by a former student that she thought the reason I had prohibited the word was because "stupid" was a curse word.

Just as firmly I believe that, indeed, it does take a village to raise a child. There is nothing more rewarding than teaching in a one-room school when the positive, cooperative spirit of family, school, and community work in unison for our most precious resource—our children, our future.

There is nothing sadder than a lack of spirit. Fortunately, teachers in recent years can reach out to more resources within the system and outside agencies for help to address some issues. Unfortunately, there is not an agency on earth that can force unwilling participants to cooperate.

Alfred's Words

Through the years I have noticed that my fellow students and I are never allowed to criticize each other in a disparaging way in front of a teacher. At the school we are taught to view the positive in everything. We are given a way to look at the world optimistically. I have sometimes heard the teachers call the entire student body "one big happy family."

*Field Trip to
Hot Springs Greenhouse*

Chapter 4
Family Values

CHAPTER 4

Family Values

Another lasting influence my parents exemplified in daily practice is that we are our brothers' and sisters' keeper. I remember the comments made many times that my parents had twelve children but raised a dozen more. Pleasant social interactions also extended into more serious concerns for everyone who shared our lives through the experience of the Great Depression of the Thirties.

My parents met the economic challenges of the time by diversifying entrepreneurship to develop an economy to support a large family and to be productive members in the community. To achieve this end my parents owned a country general store that supplied the farming community. They also had a service station supplying gas and other fuels as well as maintenance supplies. My father was also the postmaster and depot agent, which meant he maintained the train station, and met each mail and passenger train two times daily. He also met each freight train, which stopped on an irregular schedule, any time of the day or night. At one time, he even had a barbershop within the store, and he was the barber!

Family values were centrally focused when my parents became converted members of the Finnish Apostolic Lutheran Church early in their marriage. The congregation reflected the community, which was mostly Finnish. It also affected our lives culturally and economically.

Shortly after conversion my father became a lay minister. My father had a charismatic appeal and had the ability to deliver a compelling sermon. He quickly had a popular and devoted following.

In that period of our history, immigrants who found their place in our society settled in areas of compatible backgrounds and cultures. The Finnish enclaves were mainly located from the Northeast coast, the Upper Midwest, the Northwest, and the Western part of our country.

Within these groups Finnish-Americans were members of the church who still wanted their religious services performed in Finnish as well as English. Because they did not always have a Finnish-speaking minister, there was a demand for itinerant ministers. When the demand increased my father would be away from home for days and weeks at a time. By the time our younger sisters were teenagers, he retired from his other entrepreneurial activities so he could devote all his passion and energy to the church.

My mother shared the same passion my father did in living the faith they shared with unwavering devotion. I firmly believe and have often said the saddest thing that could have occurred was for my parents to have lost that faith. Not only did that faith exemplify their daily lives, but also they found comfort in the happiness it brought them. It also gave them the ability to face crises in times of sorrow with serene strength that in turn gave strength to others who shared their grief.

Besides the faith that my mother practiced, she had an added dimension of resourcefulness that reflected the lessons she learned from a childhood she experienced coming from a dysfunctional family.

꒰꒰꒰

She taught us well that you do not use it as an excuse for later lack of accomplishment and opportunity. She considered a negative approach better ignored. Instead, you should look at it as a lesson learned early. She said it strengthened the backbone and you do what you have to do. When you are met with a negative situation, you find a positive option. She told us not only to believe it, but also to believe in ourselves enough that we can turn every negative we face into a positive. You do not do it to bring glory to yourself but you do it because it is the right thing to do.

On countless occasions more frequently out of the classroom than in the classroom, I was guided by that lesson my mother taught me – *when you are faced with a negative situation, you use your time and energy to find a positive option.*

My mother had a younger sister and brother, and five older brothers. Her mother was an exceptional cook with no formal training. Yet she was able to elevate herself to a head chef position in a first class hotel. That was testimony to her talent.

My mother idolized her father who worked as a miner on the Iron Range in Minnesota and mines in Michigan. She was devastated when her parents were divorced and her mother remarried. Her relationship with her stepfather could best be described by her comment that her children would never have a stepfather. That was all I ever heard her say about it. It was an indirect reference and spoken without malice.

My grandmother's remarriage created a dysfunctional family to the extent that my mother said her only childhood memory of their home was their large dining room table surrounded by her mother's and stepfather's friends. Prohibition liquor and endless card games served as refreshment and entertainment.

To this day I do not mind a social drink on special occasions, but I do avoid drunks. To this day I am the worst card player in the world. When children were young they would groan if I volunteered to fill in when they were playing cards. And to this day I can be taught a game of cards and completely forget how to play it if a period of weeks or months lapses after I have been taught.

This has made me more empathetic when students have memory blocks, sometimes emotional, when I am teaching a concept. I can feel for them going through a similar learning problem I have already experienced.

When my mother was twelve years old, she and her older brothers came to the decision that they should take all the children and abandon their home. They moved into a cabin not too distant from their mother and proceeded to create a home where my mother and her older brothers took on all the responsibilities of a family household.

They essentially lived a subsistence lifestyle and the older brothers found odd jobs to supplement monetary necessities. My mother rarely talked about those years, and when she did, she referred to them in positive terms.

My first recollection of her reference to that period in her life was after the first and only visit my grandmother made to our home. In preparation, my mother explained that her mother's children had not lived with her for a long time. She told us my grandmother now lived several hundred miles away from us and it was too far to visit us more often. Although I was pre-school age, the visit is a still a crystal clear, vivid memory.

The only other contact my mother had with my grandmother after that was to attend her funeral. Only my parents went and on the day of their departure, we were all at school. When we came home, we found my mother had taken time to make our favorite candy. We called it "hand-pulling" taffy. She had made enough so we had something pleasant to look forward to every day when we got home from school until they came back.

Shortly after my grandmother's death, to satisfy our curiosity about their relationship, my mother described it in greater detail. The motivation they had for abandoning our grandmother was to create a more wholesome environment for the siblings and to keep them together as a family unit. There was no malice toward their mother, who relinquished all responsibility without objection, and without any further help or contact with her children.

My mother's experience had the most profound and lasting effect on me. I remember her saying she wanted us to remember this was a good example that *any time we are faced with a negative situation, we should spend our time and energy on a positive option.*

Through hard work and resolve my mother and her siblings successfully maintained an austere way of life. It was all offset by the love they shared. Recently, my nephew Danny took me to the site they lived on. It was distinguishable despite years of overgrowth and the cabin they lived in was long gone. He said he talked to elders who knew them. They told him about the Sundays when many young people regularly gathered there. They would spend the day picnicking and playing games, and then it would be back to work until the next Sunday gathering.

───

The rewards of these experiences resulted in abilities and choices that my mother instilled in her children. We were taught to make do with whatever any job or situation offered and getting it done with as little waste of time, energy, and materials in the process.

Although we lived in an environment where we could very well have run to the family store for all of our basic daily needs, life for us was quite different.

We were taught instead to take care of large gardens. We also had our own supply of dairy and meat products from our own cows, pigs, chickens, and turkeys. Hunting and fishing supplemented our needs as well, offering a leisure outlet as well as an economic benefit.

To this day, gardening is as much therapy as it is work for me and my favorite vacation is in a low-bush cranberry patch in the autumn. It is reminiscent of childhood days picking wild blueberries.

Our general store was only a source for those items we were unable to supply. In return, we developed and later came to appreciate, the worthiness of self-reliance, resourcefulness, and ingenuity.

These memories materialized into solutions on many occasions when I was challenged in a one-room school, particularly when materials and resources were not easily accessible. The greater the challenge, the greater the opportunity to nurture the potential in each of us. After all, that is what education is all about. A strong work ethic not only fosters ambition that transfers into future dreams, it also nourishes the positive attitude and sense of satisfaction that accomplishment gives. Finally, our daily activities reflect the responsibility we have, not only for our own well-being, but also for the well being of others.

Alfred's Words

During the spring and fall of our school year we have a culture camp where we participate in cultural activities. All of the students are expected to use the knowledge gained in these activities to strengthen our work ethic. Much like Gladys's gardening, fishing, and raising livestock, we are taught how to cope with the Alaskan environment.

A local wood carver, Len Palatino, worked with our students to carve an authentic portrayal of an Athabascan Chief

Chapter 5
School Values

CHAPTER **5**

School Values

Although I have divided the roots of my philosophy into three categories, Family, School, and Country, they are so intertwined from one into another it becomes difficult to separate. It is important because their affect on each other is a reminder that even though values are steadfast, there must be room for flexibility. The values are too rigid if you get caught in a mold that does not give room for growth. Flexibility and growth cannot have a source in one area without impacting all areas.

Before I ever entered school, many memories were particularly and more frequently iterations by my mother that education was the hope of the future and the answer to dreams. My mother said, "I don't know why children cry when they have to go to school. I used to cry because I couldn't."

That became my inspirational slogan. When I graduated from college with a degree in education I felt it was not only for me but for my mother as well. I have been left to wonder what dreams my mother might have realized with a formal education beyond the sixth grade one she had. That is what she sacrificed when she took on the responsibilities of making a home for her siblings at the age of twelve. With her love of children and her faith in education she would have been a great teacher. She was a great teacher despite her lack of formal training. She inspired me to bring that spirit into the classroom.

My father's influence on my educational values varied from my mother's influence. My father emigrated from Finland with a friend his age when he was eighteen years old. He had the equivalent of our high school education. Part of his education included training in vocational skills. My father was an accomplished cabinetmaker, thanks to the education he received in Finland. Although he did not choose it as a lifelong trade, he exercised his skills for his own and others' economic benefit and his own pleasure because he loved working with wood.

My father also taught me that education was a lifelong experience within and outside the walls of a formal institution. He wanted to know how equipment worked and how to repair it when it was necessary. He wanted to know how operations functioned and how to repair them when they were dysfunctional.

We were the first people in town to get electricity. I remember my father working alongside the electricians. I realized later it was not just to give a hand, but just as importantly, to learn how things work. He did this whenever the opportunity presented itself. I remember well the moment when the electrical work was complete and my father called all of us who were home at the time to come and hear him say, "I'll flick on the switch and light up our lives in more ways than one."

Another example of my father's natural talents were challenged when our radio refused to function. Instead of getting someone to repair it, my father placed the living room off limits to the smaller children and took the radio completely apart. He put each part in a designated place on the floor.

I was unaware whether he got his help from manuals, outside resources, or his own natural talents. I only know he found the problem, repaired it, and reassembled the radio. It was a floor model radio. The only difference was when he had it all together again the band worked in reverse.

We adjusted to the change and it was worth it. Keeping it in reverse was worth all the humor that it brought in conversations explaining it for the years and years it lasted.

The advent of radio had a tremendous impact in our lives. News, politics, special events, and sports were closely followed. There were times when the room would be filled with surrounding community members who could not afford the advantages of electricity and did not have radio. They would gather for special programs. President Roosevelt's fireside chats, Ed Morrow's newscasts, and Joe Louis championship fights were major attractions. We were ardent fans of Major Bowes Talent Show, comedians Jack Benny, George Burns, Fred Allen, Danny Kaye, and Red Skelton.

We were held to a hard and fast rule when it came to listening. We were told not to interrupt and to pay our full attention to the programs. In other words, our father said, "If you think your voices are more important than the one you are listening to, turn off the radio."

This training in listening skills became a valuable asset for me as a teacher and one I demanded of my students. It also helped me to recognize early in my teaching that non-verbal interruptions are just as disruptive as verbal ones and should not be tolerated. Good listeners make good students, and common courtesy is learned at the same time.

The radio was a technological advancement that expanded time and space for my world when I was growing up. It was exciting because it opened doors into borderless new frontiers. The novelty impacted my imagination more profoundly than the more advanced and sophisticated world of television and the Internet. However, I do liken the three technological "ships" of radio, television, and the Internet to Columbus and the Nina, Pinta, and Santa Maria, opening the next Age of Exploration. They are powerful tools to be treated with respect. They not only inform, they also inspire.

Radio also introduced me to my first role model in Amelia Earhart and sparked my first ambition--to become an aviatrix. At that time, whenever we heard an airplane, it would be little more than a flying spot in the distant sky. It would be an exciting moment and we would watch it until it was out of sight. I followed her career on the radio and in the press. I kept a scrapbook of her and wanted to fly just like she did.

But as it is with children, generally, my interests were diverted by other influences. The next influence was an aunt, my mother's sister, whom I dearly loved. She would entertain me with her experiences as a nurse for the doctor who delivered me. She had no formal training, but under his guidance and tutelage she assumed many of the responsibilities registered nurses had.

I set my sights even higher. Through high school I had dreams of becoming either a doctor or a psychiatrist. When I graduated at sixteen in 1941, World War II ended any chance for that dream and it was laid to rest. Realization that the lack of economic skills and lack of outside monetary assistance would create difficult if not insurmountable obstacles to overcome; I directed my ambitions elsewhere.

Enlisting in the army at a time that was to become near the end of the war gave me the opportunity to utilize the benefits provided by the GI Bill of Rights.

I realized that making money opened doors to success, so when I was discharged from the army and I could plan to have the GI Bill of Rights pay for part of my college education, I decided I would major in business administration.

Coincidentally, after I was discharged, I stopped to visit my father's sister in Massachusetts. She was a wealthy woman. When she asked me what my plans were, I told her I wanted to go to college, get a degree in business administration, and make as much money as she had. She quickly told me I did not have to do that. That is, go to college. She wanted us to enter a business partnership. She would invest in a restaurant and I would run it, and we would expand from there.

I told her I was going home to visit my family. She told me to think about it. I did not tell her then, but when I said goodbye to her I had already made up my mind. I wanted to go to college and do it my way.

When I went home to Minnesota I spent time between my family and my aunt's family. We had long talks about the future and when I mentioned I wanted to major in business administration, my aunt's husband asked me why I had chosen that field. I told him it was my opportunity to learn how to make lots of money. When he asked me what I was going to do with the money, I responded rather facetiously, "Well, I'll just count it!"

It was at that moment that I knew that my decision had a shallow base. When my uncle told me I had spent enough time with them that he felt he knew me well enough to know that money alone would not make me happy or even give me satisfaction. He thought I should reconsider my goals. Then he said I should take his suggestion into consideration, and change my major to education.

I did. I searched my soul and found the answer. In that search I remembered my father saying, in one of our dinner table discussions, that there were three great greeds that we should avoid. One was the greed for fame, the second one was the greed for power, and the third was the greed for money. It was this memory that helped me decide without any doubt that education was my major goal in college. If you are looking for fame, power, or money, you won't find it teaching.

Another factor was that I always found learning fun. In school I had not been as academically focused as I could have or should have been. I was never pressured or personally motivated enough to improve when I easily could have been. I came to regret the deficiency later, but it also made me more empathetic when I saw it in my students and I would try to find ways to help them.

While I was visiting my family, I applied and was accepted at the University of Alaska, Fairbanks. When I was a child, I avidly read about Alaska and dreamed about going there someday. When I was discharged from the army and college became my goal, I chose the University of Alaska because I felt that acceptance there would fulfill both wishes. I felt that if I went to school elsewhere, I would probably never get to Alaska.

My mother was a quiet bystander during this whole process. She waited to say it all when we said goodbye. She said that ever since I started school she knew I loved it because I would cajole playmates to "play school" after being in school all day. She told me I would have a chance to do it "for real" and she added, "Just go ahead and do it." That my mother was not able to go beyond the sixth grade gave me the added incentive to be the first in our family to graduate from college.

My father's farewell was of a different nature. My younger brother and I were traveling together by bus to Seattle, and my father was taking us to the bus station twenty miles from home. He said my departure for Alaska, separating myself from my family, reminded him of his emigration from Finland. He said that he was anxious to visit me in Alaska someday because I was moving to a place at the same latitude on the globe that he had left about the same age that I was now. He said my future looked pretty good, just like his was years earlier.

My father always liked to highlight a celebration with song--at home, in church, or in the community. So I obliged him when he asked me, "Now that you are leaving, would you sing for me one more time? I would like you to sing 'Ave Maria.'" I did.

My father made two trips to Alaska. He told us that it was the destination every young person should choose when he packs his bags and leaves home.

When I first landed in Fairbanks I felt further removed from my family than I had ever felt before. I felt so alone. I had been away from home before, but I had family nearby, except for my time in the service. Now I experienced the pangs of homesickness for the very first time. It surprised me because when I entered the army alone I did not experience these emotions.

Financially, I was relying totally on the GI Bill of Rights and a small savings account. I told myself I had only one choice and that it was success here and it was now. However, I felt like I was the ward of my government.

My adjustment to campus life was so rapid and easy that the homesickness I had felt so keenly seemed like a fleeting moment. I could not have been luckier in many ways in my choice to attend the University of Alaska. It was a small campus located about five miles from Fairbanks. Transportation consisted mainly of an hourly bus service between Fairbanks and the University and a mere handful of cars.

This helped to isolate the campus and most of one's time was spent on campus. This isolation helped to create a communal spirit. The interaction was not just between students. It included the administration, the faculty, and other workers on campus. With a few exceptions, there was a spirit of friendliness and social intermingling to a degree that I expect would be hard to find on any other campus.

There were a large number of veterans who added challenge and excitement in the classroom. On one occasion a group of us was invited to spend a social evening at a professor's home. He confessed jokingly he would be glad when we veterans would have completed our courses and graduated. He could have a greater number of young high school graduates again and would be challenged less and hopefully revered a little more.

Actually he encouraged challenges in the classroom. The respect he showed us students impressed me as much as the topic discussed. My reaction was that this was the kind of teacher I hoped I would be able to be.

My interests were in anthropology and history and I was fortunate to have the professors I had. They taught me it is just as important to make learning exciting and fun for your students, as it is to know your content material.

I wanted to become a secondary school teacher, but fate intervened. I met my future husband the first year in school. I dropped out of school for a year to work full time because my GI bill would not cover my total education. We got married the next year and went back to school. We started a family right away and having children opened a whole new world for me. The joy of learning and teaching my own children inspired me to extend that same joy teaching other younger children, and I switched my major to the elementary school program. It took me longer to get my degree but the extra courses I had already taken gave me a wider range of teaching content material. That was an advantage in a one-room school where the enrollment sometimes included high-school students.

After my third year at the University of Alaska, my husband Chuck, who wanted to become a science teacher, and I decided we needed to get a broader educational experience than the University offered. The education department had only one professor and we felt we were being inadequately prepared for our profession.

So when a high-spirited visiting professor from Chico State in California was teaching a summer course I was taking, her high expectations convinced me we had come to a crossroad. Chuck, who was working in construction that summer, and I, did a lot of soul-searching and data searching. Our final decision to continue our education at Chico State was difficult and emotional because it meant leaving Alaska for the school year. It was an economic advantage to return to Alaska each summer because Chuck could work in construction.

When we graduated three years later we had two children and were expecting our third. We also had two high-school aged nephews, Sandy and Lynn Zackowitz, who came to live with us the last year we were in Chico.

In our last year at Chico State, I was totally immersed and inspired in the environment of academia. I loved it. To take full advantage of this opportunity and fulfill the responsibilities of our growing family it became necessary for me to become more organized in my daily routine than I ever had been before. The reward was experiencing the importance that focus, energy, and organization were crucial to making situations work smoothly and effectively. Further personal proof came when I achieved my best grade point average during this same period. I knew that if I could do it in this situation, I could strive to get the same results in the classroom as long as I applied the same focus, energy, and organization that I had experienced before.

In conversations with colleagues and others, I would be asked how important the technique and methods courses I took in college were in contrast to the lessons I had learned from influences outside the classroom. My position was that my formal training was absolutely necessary as far as teaching subject material. Equally important was the ability to evaluate and value each student for what I called the "meeting of the minds."

However, the kind of teacher you are is more than the formal training you have. It is also the kind of person you are. To understand this and truly believe this was very important to me because it defended my earlier premise, we need to know where we've been to know where we are going. And indeed, we are never too old to learn or too young to teach.

Alfred's Words

The teachers here at the Gladys Dart School teach all their students to organize and focus themselves on their work. In my years here, I have taught my fellow students, though mostly the younger ones, and they have taught me things, too. Just like Gladys says, "We are never too old to learn or too young to teach."

Chapter 6
Country Values

CHAPTER 6

Country Values

As I stated earlier, I believe the cornerstones of character that built the strengths I could bring into my life as a person and particularly as a teacher were family, school, and country. I also believed these were not separate building blocks. They were instead cemented by overlapping influences that resulted in one strong foundation to build on.

Patriotism had a broader and deeper meaning than love of country. It was rooted in the proud heritage of a father who emigrated from Finland. He loved the country he left as much as he came to love the country he adopted. My mother was a second generation bicultural, bilingual Finnish-American, proud of her heritage, and nurturing that same pride in her children.

Although it was never defined in our terminology, the "melting pot" designation did not fit their model. By their example the, "mosaic" adage was more fitting. Experiences in daily life throughout my childhood molded lifelong memories and reminders that America was the answer to the hopes and dreams of immigrants. When we were given evidentiary information we were taught that there were segments of the population exposed to bias and prejudice that were distasteful ingredients in the "melting pot" or distorted the beauty of the pattern of the "mosaic." My father repeatedly said we should always look for the best in everyone and everything because "it will make you richer than money."

My teaching experience was enriched by capitalizing on the values of Native Alaskan studies in the curriculum. Unfortunately, we are still trying to recover from a period when it was excluded in our classrooms. Consequently, we have lost precious cultural enrichment that we will never be able to recover.

There was more exposure and a clearer reality of the values of patriotism I knew as a child because it occurred during the period when my father became a United States citizen. When I was going to school, civics in our social studies class became a focus for my father and became a favorite dinner table discussion

The effect on me went far beyond the dinner table. Civic-minded responsibility was instilled then and later reflected my teaching in a small school. It resulted in projects that would reflect pride in our school. It resulted in projects that extended into the community to show appreciation for their support. We did clean-up projects annually in the schoolyard, cemetery, and community before they became community-sponsored projects. We also donated large carved signs that took extensive time and effort for the students to complete because they were expected to last a long time.

Patriotism as I knew it as a child encompassed love of country expressed in terms of brotherhood and duty. In celebration, the Fourth of July was the most popular and favorite holiday of the year including Christmas. The games and fireworks were great, but it was the political speaker who highlighted the day's activities who we remembered most.   In the line of duty, the events of history changed the course of our future because World War II was imminent. I had wondered where my father's loyalty would lie if he were forced to choose between Finland and America. He gave me the answer when he came rushing into our home when he had heard the news of the Pearl Harbor disaster. In emotional terms he announced the news. In the next breath he wished out loud that he could enlist and serve our country as a chaplain. I never wondered where my father's loyalties were after that incident.

Although my father did not serve in World War II, six of the twelve children did. Those that did not and who were old enough to be in the work force worked in jobs related to the war effort. Sacrifices were expected and met at home as well as on the front because it was our patriotic duty. Government imposed rationing of gasoline and sugar is an example. We were expected to sacrifice pleasure for austerity and donate what we could for the war such as Care Packages. My contribution was to work as a riveter on B-17's and B-29's for Boeing.

When we lost our oldest brother in France in 1944, I decided to enlist. A friend and I went to Seattle. We went to the Marine recruiting office, but it was closed. We went to the U.S. Navy recruiting office and they were closed. So we went to the Army recruiting office. They were open. My friend was rejected. I wasn't, and I left the office ready to serve my country in the Medical Corps.

I completed an intensive medical technician's course in Indiana after basic training in Iowa. After that assignment, we were transferred to Miami Beach in Florida. My service in the medical area was cut short because I was transferred to the Air Force where my work was finalizing medical and service records of overseas soldiers who were recovering patients or freed prisoners of war and were getting prepared for their discharge from the service. Our unit's next transfer was to North Carolina. We were slated for an overseas assignment. The assignment was cancelled because the war came to a close. My final transfer was to Fort Dix where I was discharged eighteen months after my enlistment. My service to my country was rewarded with the gift of the GI Bill of Rights and the opportunity to pursue my hopes and dreams.

Alfred's Words

Gladys's love of her country has indeed endured over the years in my school. For example, we have a school luncheon on the anniversary of 9/11/2001 to commemorate those who lost their lives that day. We invite community members and do special things like honor heroes of 9/11 or ask the elders of the village to share their experience with war. The community in Manley Hot Springs is very patriotic. During these events with the school children they pass their patriotism on to the next generation.

Our students made this sign as a show of appreciation to the community

Part 2 - In Deed

Sharing is the essence of teaching. It is, I have come to believe, the essence of civilization… Without it, the imagination is but the echo of the self, trapped in a soundproof chamber, reverberating upon itself until it is spent in exhaustion or futility."

                        Bill Moyers
                        U.S. Journalist

Chapter 7
Reestablishing Manley Hot Springs School

CHAPTER 7

Reestablishing Manley Hot Springs School

I had a year of teaching experience in Fairbanks before my one-room teaching experience in Manley Hot Springs. It was the same year we purchased the hot springs property in Manley Hot Springs in 1955. I had already signed a contract to teach in Fairbanks where I would teach first grade in the basement of the University Presbyterian Church in the College area. Since I had signed the contract prior to our property purchase, I stayed and taught in Fairbanks that year. Chuck came to Manley Hot Springs and started work on our first greenhouse, where he planned to grow tomatoes, cucumbers, eggplant, and melons commercially.

I had a wonderful experience teaching that first year. It turned out it was a great benefit, not only for me as far as my experience as a teacher, but it also became a value to me after I arrived in Manley Hot Springs.

The Superintendent of Schools in Fairbanks was Dr. Ryan and he was the one who hired me for the position in the College area. My Principal was Mr. Cheney. When they assigned me to teach first grade in the College area I was happy to do that because we had lived in the College area and we knew many families who lived there.

They had had a problem with the school the year before and they said they wanted me to know that. I was grateful for that information. For that reason, I asked if I could speak with the parents and the community at the first PTA meeting at the beginning of the year. I think it is very important for the teachers to reach out to the parents and the community. I also think it is just as important for the community to reach out to the school and to be in close, sustained communication with each other.

It was in that spirit that I spoke at that meeting. I introduced myself as a first year teacher. I spoke briefly of my philosophy of education. I told them how grateful I was to teach at the first grade level because it was the children's first introduction into education. The challenge for me was to instill a love of learning as they developed the necessary self-discipline and work skills to meet my high expectations of their potential.

I told them about certain techniques in my teaching. An example of this was to tell the parent that the best way to help their child was to be in very close contact with the teachers in the school, find out how and why they are teaching a certain technique or the sequence used in teaching a concept. In that way, they can reinforce the concept when their children ask for help with their homework. There should always be room for flexibility so suggestions from students, parents, or teachers, will be considered in the learning experience. Communication is crucial in this cooperative process. I also welcomed and encouraged parents to come in to confer with or without the student whenever they wanted to. I also encouraged them to visit school announced or unannounced. Good things happen when there is communication, communication, and communication.

I would see Dr. Ryan briefly during the school year and the occasions were always professional and inspiring. At the end of a successful school year I was very anxious to get to Manley Hot Springs. We had three small children and had to move everything we owned from Fairbanks. I was able to arrive in Manley Hot Springs the week after school was out.

When I arrived in Manley Hot Springs, Jim was nineteen months old, John was three and Diane was five. And there was no school. There were only two other children; Mary and Billy Lanning, so there were five children in the entire town. There were only fifteen people living in Manley Hot Springs the winter of '56-'57. We settled in and I taught Diane by using correspondence courses, which were offered to children when no school was within a reasonable range for that year and the next.

We had purchased the property from Bob Byers, the local bush pilot. He and his wife did not want to teach their children at home by correspondence, so they moved the family into town. They then decided it was not going to work because the family was not together most of the time. They decided to sell the bush pilot business to Frank Jones, who was a pilot in their employ. Frank Jones is a very, very special person when it comes to education in Manley Hot Springs. It was in early summer in 1958 when he and his wife Hazel came to the house to visit and he asked, " Now what would it take to start a school in Manley Hot Springs?" I said I did not know, but I could certainly find out what was required to do that.

Frank said he wanted us to know that there were people who wanted to come and move to Manley Hot Springs, but they felt they could not because they had children and there was no school. He also said he was thinking of his business. He knew that if Manley Hot Springs grew so would his business grow.

I knew that Dr. Ryan, who had hired me as a teacher in Fairbanks, was now the Commissioner of Education for the State of Alaska in Juneau. So I wrote to the Department of Education. I asked the department what requirements had to be met to make our school become a reality. They said that it would take ten children to be categorized as a special school. It would take a certified teacher and the community would have to supply the building. We suggested using an extra 16X20 foot cabin we had on the property if it would meet the standard. So the first step was taken to the establishment of the school in Manley Hot Springs.

The State Board of Education had a meeting. We were grateful to Dr. Ryan for being there as the Commissioner of Education. He helped us in presenting our case to them. When we described the building the Board accepted that. Some people from the Department of Education came to Manley Hot Springs to inspect the building. Chuck told them that we would not have electricity, but we would have Coleman lanterns. We would not have plumbing, but we would have an outhouse. We would have hot water heat in the school. We passed inspection.

Chuck offered rent for the building, maintenance, and custodial services for one hundred dollars a month. The department accepted the offer. So here it was August and school would start the day after Labor Day. We did not have any furniture or blackboards, and we did not have any supplies or materials.

Chuck found two large old tables. They were handmade by some local in the past to serve as worktables. Chuck sandpapered them until they were usable. For the smaller children he cut part of the legs off to accommodate for the size of the students. He collected "Blazo" boxes. They were wooden shipping containers built especially to fit two five-gallon tin cans of fuel. They were sturdy enough and with a cushion to cover them, they were comfortable enough to substitute for a chair. This was more practical than a bench because they could also use the boxes for storage of personal items.

Chuck also purchased two pieces of 4X8 foot plywood boards and painted them with black slate paint to serve as our blackboards. I had pastel chalk and I wrote the letters of the alphabet in cheerful colors at the top of each blackboard and drew a picture to go with each one to be used later teaching beginners reading. The only other audio-visual tool I had was an old globe I had at the house. I still have that globe and I treasure it dearly.

While Chuck was getting the building ready, the community came to my rescue supplementing our personal supply with an assortment of paper, pencils, chalk, crayons, and other materials I might be able to use. We had an extensive personal library. I was able to use our old college texts for teaching reference.

Other books gave us a wide selection in the area of language arts mainly, as well as other areas of the curriculum. Missing were the children's textbooks needed to meet the curricular goals. They were being shipped by boat.

They said our supplies would arrive on the last boat, but it wasn't due for more than a month. So I had to do most of my teaching outside. I capitalized on the richness of our natural world as a classroom. I had them outside as much as I had them inside. What they learned outside they brought inside.

When the boat came in you would have thought it was Christmas, not just for the children at school, but every family in town. Families that did not have children were as excited the rest of us when the boat came in. As soon as that boat landed, volunteers with trucks brought the equipment to the school. The desks were not assembled. I thought I had to find someone to put all this furniture together. The next morning, I was at school before 7:00 AM. To my surprise, a bachelor in town named Ed Lawler was already there with his carpenter tools. He was there every day before 7:00 and worked all day until every piece of equipment was assembled. Some children started coming early just to watch and help, so we promised them they could choose their own desks. That is how we reestablished the school in Manley Hot Springs.

School was held in the building for three years. The enrollment had increased to nineteen. The Department of Education decided the building was too small to accommodate them safely. When we had our last Christmas program we had to plan it so that the children would remain on the stage the whole time. Once the audience was seated there was not any room for the children to exit the stage during the program.

When conditions became that crowded, indeed, it was time to move. The building is still there and is fondly called, "The Old School."

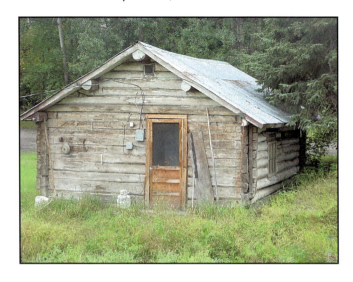

Alfred's Words

This entire year our school theme has been Gladys Dart School history. The Old School, the school after that, part of the current school, and the current school have all been researched by the students this year. In a writing session with Gladys we discussed the nicknames of these schools. The Old School is sometimes called the "Moldy Moldy," the second school the "Oldy Moldy," the first part of the current school the " Oldy Goldy," and the school I attend the "Goldy Goldy." I am not sure when or where these nicknames arose, but often a student is told to head out to the "Oldy Moldy," where the school stores old odds and ends they no longer need, to retrieve something. The history of the Gladys Dart School is a rich one that I am glad to be studying.

The Oldy Moldy 1963 - 1980

Chapter 8
Learning and Teaching in a One-Room School

CHAPTER 8

Learning and Teaching in a One-Room School

Home is where the heart is. Having received my elementary education in a one-room school, I felt like I was coming home when I started teaching in a one-room school. With my personal experience as a student in a one-room school, together with my professional training, I was fortunate to experience the unique answers one could not find in any other setting.

One of these answers defined my perception as well as my description of a one-room school. For me, a one-room school is analogous to a microcosm of society. My responsibility was to recognize and help each child reach his or her greatest potential in the context of differences in gender, age, ability, and personal and cultural background. You learn to play together, work together, and learn together in a safe and happy environment. It also fostered leadership and freedom beyond the exclusivity of classrooms of peers. It was citizenship in action every day.

Gender, age, and ability had to be considered in the physical education program in a one-room school when they did it together. They were also key determiners in the sports and leisure time activities. These were the same things I had to consider as a child in a large home and a small community and as an elementary student in a one-room school.

Fairness ruled the day in a small community where a team of peers could not be created. To compensate for it, the unspoken rule for it was that captains had to choose their players so that each team was equal in gender, age, and ability.

For example, we loved football, and for some reason it was not touch football. When the game involved peers it was no-holds-barred, but when gender, age, and ability became a factor, when a big person tackled a small person it was more like a big hug than a tackle.

Because my childhood team sports included a range in gender, age, and, ability, I was able to supply the same standard more confidently when I was teaching team sports. Rules had to be flexible for team members to accommodate these differences. For example, beginners in softball were given six strikes and then they were reduced as their ability improved. The players determined the rule changes to insure fairness and good sportsmanship. A competitive spirit developed despite the odds.

Ingenuity and improvisation solved the lack of equipment or participation. When I was a child some of the children in the community wanted to ski, but did not have the equipment. Since we were still in a depression economy adults came forth and contributed their time and talents and made skis from local trees. A similar situation occurred when I was teaching. Some students wanted to learn how to ski. We did not have money in the budget. Some surplus army skis were donated by a community member who knew of our predicament. He made the extra effort to get the skis. With extra volunteer help the skis were altered in size and shape for the students.

When I was a child adults sometimes participated in games but, mostly they were very supportive fans. These activities also provided free entertainment when there was little money to spend. They cheered us in various group and individual competition. I found this same thing to be true in our community when I started to teach. The ultimate benefit was building athletic skills and promoting sportsmanship. The similarities between my childhood experience and the physical education program in a one-room school was so striking that I sometimes felt like I was reliving the past.

The philosophy in the methods classes at Chico State in the area of physical education was an added emphasis. We were taught to regard physical education with an emphasis on the individual in the development of skills and sportsmanship. Equality was rated on the basis of meeting one's potential to level the playing field in individual or team competition.

Limited classroom space and no gym in most of my teaching experience factored into the need that games were mostly playground activities. I went out with the children during their mid-morning and mid-afternoon recesses, and during their lunch break. Sometimes it was in the role of a supervisor. Sometimes it was in the role of a player depending on the type of activity the children chose, but I was always the umpire.

There were reasons for my participation other than the fact that I enjoyed playing with them as much as I enjoyed watching them interact. The way children related to each other gave me helpful information and insight to interaction I could use to an advantage in the classroom. It was especially helpful in those projects when you paired an older student with a younger student working together. We did this often. It offered the chance for me to see them grow in their athletic skills. More importantly, it offered the opportunity to teach the value of sportsmanship, and not only how it adds to the enjoyment of the game, but also the way we treat ourselves and others in moments of victory or defeat. It also gives the awareness that inclusion, despite gender, age, or ability makes good sportsmen and better citizens.

Because individual, intellectual, and behavioral expectations are so central to every aspect of teaching it did not take long to recognize that teaching is as much an art as it is a science. I realized this when I had developed a technique that worked well enough to think it was the perfect answer. Then I would get a student whose understanding was on a wavelength either above or below mine. The technique was derailed and what I attribute to as artistry saved the day. The search by the teacher and the student until the same wavelength was found and inspired excitement in the classroom. Those moments made me thankful I had chosen teaching as a career.

In learning subjects as diverse as sports and literature, it is critical how important our expectations are. In these areas, as well as all areas of learning, there were the recurring examples left to remind me that too often we underestimate the intellectual potential and high expectations that our children are capable of achieving. On the other hand we too often place restrictions on their behavior and we do not let children be children. The shy withdrawn child who is hesitant to express him or herself was a far greater concern to me than the free spirit in the classroom.

Alfred's Words

Since Gladys started the school, we have expanded a little and have a gym, but we always go outside when we can. In the spring and fall when we have school we are outside for a good bit of time each day, using the little warm weather that we have for outdoor activities. Through these outdoor activities I have learned the values of sportsmanship and have had lots of fun in the process. This is one instance showing that anything can teach you a lesson.

New School First Phase 1980

Our school today!

Chapter 9
Starting Classroom Traditions

CHAPTER **9**

Starting Classroom Traditions

The school newspaper, the "Manley Highlights", was developed as a medium to facilitate the relationship between our territorial school and the community the first year the classroom was reestablished in 1958. It encouraged and insured ongoing involvement of the community in the school and the school in the community. Community support fosters better schools. School support fosters better communities.

The first step in setting up the newspaper was to have a contest to name it and design the logo. It was a big deal and created excitement with students and that excitement extended to the community.

The first Gladys Dart School newspaper, before the title was selected. Thus the question marks.

A student won the contest! The winner was chosen by a committee of three people who decided on their choice pulling the winner's name from a container. Judges included one student and two community members. They chose their own judging strategy that was kept secret by the committee. The design of the northern sun signified the rising of education in Manley Hot Springs. It is still used with some variations, but with the same significance.

The next step was to decide how often the newspaper should be published. The students decided to do it weekly. We used a technology of the day called the hectograph. It was a wooden tray that contained a gel that would duplicate a stencil of each page of the paper. It was a slow, tedious process, because each sheet would have to be placed very carefully on the gel long enough to absorb the image. It had to be as carefully removed so the gel would not be disturbed and ruin the image. The printing was done outside of school hours because it was such a slow process, but the paper always met the deadline.

The next printing technology that became available was the ditto machine. It was a blessing because it reduced the amount of time it took to print the paper. You attached a stencil to a drum containing the duplicating fluid. Turning a crank completed the process. Students started taking greater responsibility for the printing. They had full responsibility for writing the articles and making stencils.

Then came the electric ditto machine. Instead of a crank, all you had to do was press a button. The only change was an increased speed of the printing process. As there had always been a race to volunteer to turn the crank, it now became a race to press the button.

The next advancement was the Xerox machine. For the first time the maintenance of the machines had to be considered. We weren't trained to do this so technicians from out of town had to come when the machines required adjustment or repair. I recall one technician telling me it would be to our advantage economically not to buy the first models of a new product. Ensuing models would have many of the kinks worked out, and his services would not be required as often. Since services required more time in travel and expenses, I appreciated his advice. Taking into account the advantages it gave students and their education; I felt it was worth the price to get an original as long as we could afford it.

Then, finally came the computer. This was mostly after I had retired. I have enjoyed its potential utilized in the publication of the "Manley Highlights", which is still available, and I enjoy in my retirement. With each progressive stage student responsibility for the paper increased. During the whole process the content was always the full responsibility of the students.

Every student was expected to work on the content. Articles would be chosen or the student would be assigned one. We were also very fortunate when community members voluntarily submitted articles.

We helped pay for the publication through subscriptions. At first it was just a local production, but it quickly expanded. We began sending a free copy to each school in the district and to the District Office. This meant that the mailing costs increased from local to outside subscribers. We have also had a few international subscribers.

჻჻჻

The students also printed special sections like letters to the editor and the weekly hot lunch menu. It created its own moments of amusement. Once when we had Pilot Bread, which is a large cracker still available in stores, on the lunch menu list several times, it prompted a letter to the editor asking us for a recipe for that "bread for pilots."

The goal was to have the children involved as much as possible. The students used to deliver locally to save mailing cost until it became a safety issue. The time it took away from home and their chores, dark days, and inclement weather became issues of enough concern we opted for mail delivery.

The "Manley Highlights" inspired the yearbook. Dixie Dayo, a student, asked why we did not have a yearbook. It is another example how wonderful projects originate with student ideas. Rewards from producing a newspaper inspired creativity that could be incorporated into the curriculum. It also taught the students setting and maintaining deadlines, responsibility for business contracts with the subscribers, and it set and maintained a historical record of our school and community. The yearbook is still published annually.

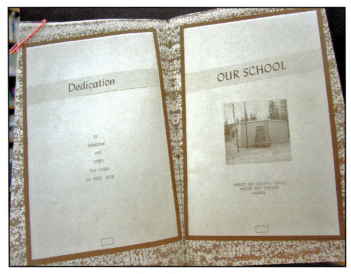

Our Yearbook
Memories and Treasures
Through the years

If this lesson teaches us anything, it is that any school publication can keep a record that benefits the whole school district. It was not thought of or promoted at the time, but this is another reason each school in the district should do its own newspaper; to become part of the school district's archives, serving as information and entertainment for others as it has for us.

Certain creative projects became traditions because they not only met curricular requirements; they could be accomplished best in a one-room school in a small village. An example of this was our annual homemade movie that we presented during our Christmas program.

The idea originated with a unit on poetry, which is part of the language arts curriculum. It gave the opportunity to teach the elements of poetry. We chose "'Twas the night before Christmas'" because it translated so well into the theme of the Christmas program.

Student consensus decided that the children from each family would create a verse and illustration portraying a memorable event that occurred in their family during the year. Students with parents had the full responsibility for the decision for their family. Community members without students were decided by volunteers or group discussion to insure that no one would be left out. Help was accepted from anyone at any time.

The same rules applied to the art that depicted each verse. An older child chose or was assigned to a younger child and they were primarily responsible, but could seek and accept help when needed. The final project was put on a roller and students took turns reading each section when it was presented during the Christmas program. We called it "'Twas the year before Christmas, and all through Hot Springs." Most importantly, it was a beautiful expression of who we were and where we came from. It is still an annual tradition. Now it is totally done on the computer, although the children still read the verses. It also has become a permanent historical record of our town for that year.

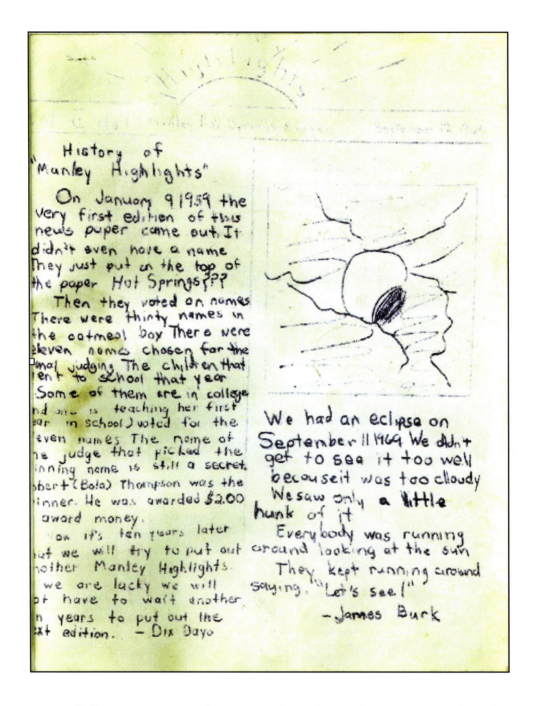

An article by Dixie Dayo and James Burk on the tenth anniversary of the first Manley Highlights release.

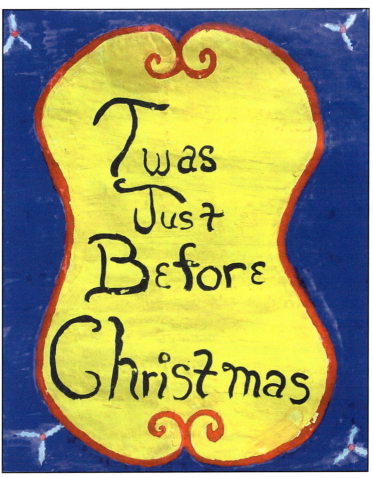

The very beginning and end of our traditional Christmas movie.

IN DEED INDEED

> Susan has been busy this Holiday Season,
> Spending time with Dave for some super reason.
> Between making plans for a grand old wedding,
> They are still having time to go dog sledding.

To Susan Butcher and David Monson, whose support we appreciated through the years

STARTING CLASSROOM TRADITIONS

Cy likes Hawaii and he's planning to go there,
Daisy's likes differ and she doesn't quite know where,
To go this winter — so her plans are a battle,
We think she likes the West — cinched in the saddle.

Cy and Daisy Hetherington sold a parcel of their land to the state to build the Oldy Moldy and the Goldy Goldy. They have always been supporters of the school. Daisy's love of history developed a dedication to education in our community. Her patriotism was most clearly shown when the September 11, 2001 attack on the United States occurred. She came down to the school that very morning, a couple of hours after the attack, and marched through the school giving each student a small United States flag and said to 'pray for those people and our country'. She said this with a tear in her eyes. We will never forget that act of patriotism by Daisy.

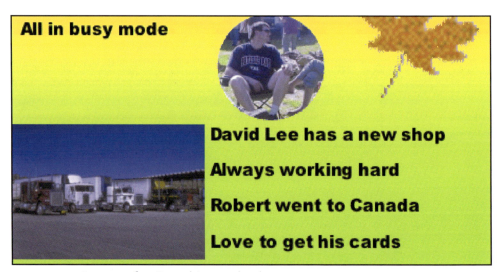

A poem for David Lee, who leaves us many memories

This poem was made for Joee Ray, who inspired the title of this book, and always let us know when good things happen

Alfred's Words

Through the years of attending the Gladys Dart School, from kindergarten to 10th grade, the newspaper, town poem, and yearbook have been major parts of my education. Every month we are expected to write an article, edit peer articles, organize these articles into the newspaper, and finally print and collate the Manley Highlights. It has been good way for me to learn responsibility and has helped me hone my writing skills. Midway through the year we all write up a small poem about what we and our families have done through the year from the last town poem to the current one.

We are also expected to write poems for every family in the community. These poems have helped me learn the importance of archiving local history and, more importantly, has given me a sense of community involvement. After every year of school my peers and I create our yearbook pages, sometimes looking back through the newspapers and town poems for inspiration. These three writing activities that take me through the year have been important to me as a student at the Gladys Dart School.

School Christmas Program

Chapter 10
Facing the Challenges of Inadequacy

CHAPTER **10**

Facing the Challenges of Inadequacy

Teachers, as all adults, I am sure, feel inadequacies in the fulfillment of their responsibilities as role models or as teachers. This is especially true when mastery of knowledge is a basic criterion for success. It is true when a teacher is responsible for teaching one subject area as they are in many large schools. The issue is compounded when a teacher is responsible for all subject areas as they are in teaching in one-grade situations. The challenges in a one-room school are even greater when one teacher is responsible for all subject areas in a multi-grade situation.

Fortunately, resourcefulness, ingenuity, and creativity actively pursued and exercised will help to find answers and solutions for the lack of a teacher's expertise. So it was with my lack of expertise teaching music. The first step was to admit and confront the extent of my own inadequacies. Searching for solutions was an education in itself. It not only taught me there were countless opportunities to not only do a better job teaching in those areas where you were inadequate, it also enriched areas where you felt confident.

I felt my inadequacy as a teacher in the area of music more keenly because I really loved music, particularly singing, which was such an enjoyable part of my childhood.

My elementary school education experience in music did not go beyond informal group singing on occasion. It was not even taught at the level of choir singing. There was no instruction in instrumental music due to budgetary restrictions created by the Great Depression. We did have a piano, but I had only one elementary teacher who played it. With her we had many memorable hours of singing. Our teacher would open the windows facing the community because someone who lived close to the school in our small town said our voices reached out loud and clear for their enjoyment, too.

IN DEED INDEED

I was looking forward to music instruction in high school, but when the music teacher found out I could not read music, he said I was too far behind the others and he did not have the time for individual attention.

In college, an elementary music methods course in sight singing was the only preparation I had for teaching music. It was a meager background to institute music instruction for students in a one-room school. So I started with singing. We learned a variety of patriotic songs first, including "Alaska's Flag", our state song. Children took weekly turns raising the flag and then coming in and choosing a patriotic song after they led the Pledge of Allegiance to the flag that was on permanent display in the classroom. After the outside flag was lowered and folded at the end of the day we spent a short period before children were dismissed for the day when they would choose songs from all-time favorites they were learning. Weeks before Christmas in the morning and at the end of the day we would turn all the lights off except for the ones on the Christmas tree. We would sit around the tree and children would choose favorite carols they had learned.

I found instruments in the early years that my limited knowledge could handle. We purchased recorders, tambourines, rhythm sticks, triangles, and an auto-harp. My favorite resource was an album produced by RCA Victor called "Music for Rhythm Bands." Before and during the introduction to the instruments, rhythmic activities added fun in learning what music was all about. Examples we used were free body expressions like swaying and clapping.

Another example was imitative play like galloping horses, dancing snowflakes, or whirling gypsies. These activities freed inhibitions through music expression. Another example was dramatization when it related to stories expressed in music. The children mastered the instruments enough to perform in school programs. But I felt with good reason that they thought of these instruments as musical toys rather than musical instruments. I also felt it was a reflection of my own struggles.

I was more successful in the area of music appreciation. Thanks again to another album RCA recorded for Reader's Digest called "Music of the World's Great Composers." Not only did it introduce the students to the classics in literature, it also introduced them to the musical interpretations, especially opera, symphony, and classical music. It also inspired dramatic play and art interpretations regardless of grade level. I was as much a student as I was a teacher at the time.

The moment of greatest gratitude came when there was enough money in the school budget as a result of the development of the state's oil resources and the building of the Alaska pipeline. After careful research and other considerations, I purchased a set of hand bells. Upon the advice of the company I purchased them from, I did not purchase the smallest or the largest bells. I could not express my gratitude enough for the honesty and generosity of their advice, because they were expensive, and the ones we purchased served our needs adequately.

It served us adequately in two ways. On one hand, with my own limitations teaching music, teaching the subject with hand bells gave me a greater measure of comfort and pleasure of achievement. On the other hand, it was an opportunity to include all the students to participate as a group at the same time. It resulted in performances in programs throughout the year and it was also popular in annual spring festivals our school district held for many years.

Later a gifted teacher and colleague, Damaris Mortvedt, introduced a successful music program for her students. She convinced the parents and the Community School Committee that she could institute piano lessons to all students if the money could be transferred from the lunch program. They agreed and the students were rewarded with piano lessons and learning the universal language of music.

In retirement, I enjoy listening to musical programs at school and how music reflects its importance in the daily curriculum. It is also a reflection how important and crucial music and all arts are in the educational process to develop our students' full potential.

As it turned out, I was grateful for my musical inadequacies because the lessons I learned trying to solve them I could extend into other areas where I felt more confident in my ability to teach.

I became more aware and took more advantages of the resources that were available, particularly on a volunteer basis. When we invited a geologist, David Hopkins, we collected rocks on a field trip that he said were probably a million years old. The children treated them like treasures. He also lectured on his theory that our state once had a land bridge to Russia. This excited the imagination of our students.

When a nephew, Sandy Zackowitz, came for a week's visit he volunteered to give concentrated ski lessons with successful results.

When itinerants like counselors, state troopers, and public health nurses came to our village I invited them to come to school and get to know each student personally so the students would know people like these were always there to help them anytime should the occasion arise.

And we were always looking for and sometimes found artists and musicians--local, transient, or funded through special projects--who would volunteer and enrich the school program.

We were also aware that some of our richest resources lived with us. We had Elizabeth Fleagle, a vivacious, intelligent Eskimo, who shared her cultural

IN DEED INDEED

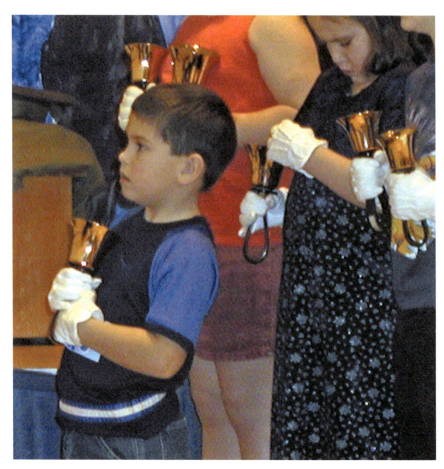

expertise and active support of our school tirelessly. We also have Judy Woods, an Athabaskan elder, who shares her rich cultural heritage and is still active in her participation at school. Finally, we had Sally Hudson, an Athabaskan, who was born and raised in our region. She shared her rich historical and cultural knowledge when she volunteered her services. She developed a mini-course that touched every aspect of her culture. She explained her young life in a subsistence lifestyle. She brought in toys made from bone that she had saved from her childhood because in those days there were no stores to buy them from. She touched on the respect her people had for the land and the ecological practices to prove it. She touched upon her language so we were able to read a short story in Athabaskan when the mini-course was over. We translated the carol, "O Come All Ye Faithful" and sang it in Athabaskan for several years as part of our Christmas program. She described clothes made from animal skins and beadwork that decorated them. She came dressed in full native ceremonial regalia when we had a potlatch that celebrated the end of the course. She also taught the children the song of the robin, saying it was much longer when she was a child, but, as she explained, in modern times everything seems to go by faster and shorter.

We held a contest most of the early years I taught and whoever saw or heard the first robin in spring won. It was, to my delight, a year later after Sally's course when a student, Frank Fleagle, came running into the school shortly after I arrived and he burst out with arms wide open, "Mrs. Dart! Mrs. Dart! I won!" and he burst out singing Sally's song of the robin.

A highlight for me was the day I recognized my students had also discovered the value of educational resources. Our school had outhouse facilities. Children would write their names on the board when they needed to use it, so only one student would be out of the classroom at a time, and they did not require my permission to leave.

Jay deLima had gone out and when he was coming back he saw four strangers walking on the road by the school. He ran to them and found out they were visitors from Germany. He invited them to come in to our school and when they were reluctant he insisted. He brought them in and we all introduced ourselves to each other. I put the daily lesson plans aside and asked them to join us. At the end of a couple of hours, we had learned about each other and the information covered a good part of what our curriculum directed us to teach.

When I reflected on what had happened at the end of the day, I felt we had learned a lot more from each other than the information we had exchanged.

Another good day in school was over.

Indeed.

Alfred's Words

Feeling inadequate can be a struggle for anyone, but when you feel that you cannot help those who need it, the stress can bear down on you. However, this can also help some people become more creative and efficient when the situation is overwhelming. I believe this is exemplified in this chapter.

Music
Music
Everywhere

Chapter 11
Reading

CHAPTER 11

Reading

Reading is the master key to learning. A teacher's joy to hear children read the first time is equivalent to the joy parents feel when they hear their child speak their first words. There is no greater satisfaction for a teacher than to know a student has learned something new.

My love for literature goes back farther than my memory. We read and we were read to. When books were not always available due to the Great Depression storytelling based on reality or creativity was a favorite pastime.

As a parent, I relived my past. I started to read to my children before they were born. Before they learned to talk and when they were learning to talk, I used large picture books. They learned to identify the picture and to identify words and I would sometimes create a little story to add humor or pique interest to make it easier to remember. By the time they entered school they had their favorite children's stories that ranged from nursery rhymes, fables, fairytales, and legends from North American Indian, to Greek, Roman, and Norse myths.

I was able to relive it again as a teacher, especially in the years before television, the Internet, and other advances in technology competed for time in the classroom. The story hour highlighted the period right after lunch.

I chose the books or stories from books unless it was a special request from a student or students. My very favorite resource for reading was a children's anthology text from a college course in literature. It contained a range wide enough to help me teach appreciation of literature. I also liked that particular textbook because it did not contain any pictures. I demanded uninterrupted attention that had been demanded from me years before when the radio was introduced in our home. If there was a verbal or nonverbal interruption, I would simply stop reading, and in complete silence I would look at my students. When I had their full attention I would continue reading. I can remember times when other students who were not pleased at the interruption would also give disapproving looks. It was very effective. In all those years, there was only one time it didn't work. Then I just closed the book, put it away and without one word resumed the next class.

I also wanted confirmation that the children comprehended the literature session. So after each story hour, I assigned an art lesson that depicted some part of the story. They could work on it in their spare time until the next story hour. Sometimes I would ask for something specific. For example, I would ask them to draw a picture of their favorite character, or I would ask them to draw a picture of a specific event, or I would ask them to draw a scene or activity that they especially liked or did not like. At other times, the illustration could be entirely their choice. Before we started the next day's story hour, each child would display his or her work and the others would have to identify it or explain it. This gave me an opportunity to evaluate their listening skills and their comprehension. It also gave the students a way to express their appreciation in a different medium. I also believed it honed their listening and art skills.

There was one area I assigned as an art assignment that was my favorite. When I read a story that showed a strong emotion such as happiness, sorrow, fear, bravery, strength, or weakness, I would ask them to illustrate the emotion. The abstract artwork this produced caused a response in me I cannot yet fully describe. I can only say it brought out emotions of wonder, as strong or stronger than any I had asked them to portray. My only regret is that I did not ask them if I could keep them for myself in a portfolio with an anecdotal record to keep in the archives at school. But each student had his own art portfolio at school that he or she took home at the end of the year. I want to believe that they went where they belonged.

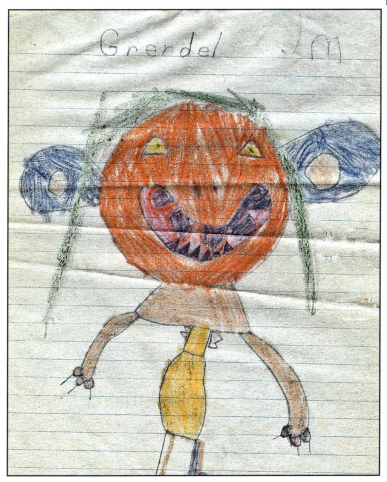

Grendel, the monster from Beowulf, done by James Dart in the 1st grade.

Diane Dart's rendering of Pele, the Hawaiian legend

Two of Diane Dart's free choice drawings. The colors of the drawing on the right were used to show emotion.

IN DEED INDEED

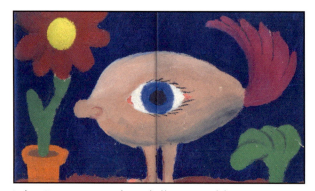

John Dart created and illustrated his own story.

THE SEED
I come from a seed. You don't know who I am or what I am,
and I can't tell because I don't have a mouth.

Alfred's Words

The Gladys Dart School teaches students that reading is an important part of their education. I was taught in school to be a good reader with programs like Battle of the Books. Since I read my first book of over 300 pages in 1st grade I have challenged myself to read at the highest level I can manage. I think Gladys did very well to address the importance of reading.

Robert Lee reading at Awards Night with Mrs. Wright

Chapter 12
Testing

CHAPTER **12**

Testing

Testing is a valuable tool in helping us do our job in the classroom. It also tells us how well we are doing that job. Testing comes in many forms: oral, nonverbal, written, daily quizzes, and standardized tests, which become a permanent record in every child's personal folder. Although we teachers do the bulk of the testing, we also use psychologists and other professionals who are qualified to evaluate for specific objectives.

All of these are crucial in helping us know our students better. They open avenues to establish a rapport and relationship with students so they can acquire the knowledge it is our primary duty to deliver. The proficiency in subject content we require is reflected in test results. To help students reach their greatest potential, however, requires much more than passing a test.

The standardized tests were effective aids for me in the small one-room school setting. Having the same students over a period of years was another advantage. Living as a neighbor and friend and having a closer relationship with them was also an advantage. The better you know the student, the easier it is to teach him or her.

A student comes to school affected by events, positive or negative, that are happening inside as well as outside the school that will influence his performance in school. During the period of standardized test taking, particularly, I would take this into special consideration. Both students and parents alike were made aware of the importance and permanency of these test results in their personal folders. So I stressed the importance that they come to school well rested, well fed, and in the best frame of mind. Special plans were also made to offer pleasant entertaining diversions between tests because it created an atmosphere that test taking could be a fun time as well.

In my experience, standardized tests also became a tool to evaluate me as a teacher as well. It could be done in a one-room school in a way it could not have been done in a larger school where your student body changes every year. When I analyzed the results and realized there was a lower performance in a particular area with the whole group, I would question myself as far as the type of job I was doing. For example, there was one time when I noticed in the particular section of maps, charts, and graph skills (in the area of study skills) many students performed lower than I knew they were capable of. So I knew it was probably in the way I had been teaching them. I concentrated extra effort, brought in extra resources, and emphasized more content, and as a result I noticed an improvement the next year when they took the test. I also took special notice when an individual student performed lower than I knew he was capable of and I would take the same remedial steps.

In the few years when I taught in a one-class large school situation, I found the standardized tests useful in getting ready for the school year. My highest priority was to spend most of my time in preparation by studying the personal folders of my students. The information was a helpful introduction and I felt I had already met and engaged with my students before I first saw them.

There was a time when the IQ tests teachers gave were a part of every child's record. I could not understand and I objected to the decision to stop using them. For me it became another missing link in helping me know my student better. I felt strongly the more I knew of the mental capacity, aptitude capabilities, physical abilities, and relevant background influences the easier it was to understand and teach my students. Testing provides some answers and provokes questions to look for more answers.

There was also a time when teachers left anecdotal records in each student's permanent folders. When they no longer permitted that practice, I felt I had lost another link to knowing my student better. Whether the information was good or bad, I wanted to know. Whether it was a former teacher's perception, I needed to know. Whether it was some event or experience in or out of school, that had an impact great enough to become a part of the student's record, I needed to know. It was my duty to gain insight without passing judgment and to respond accordingly.

Alfred's Words

I still use tests for most of my classes, although that is not very unusual in a school. Some people take tests better or worse than others and it will not be a sure indication of who is smarter. I am glad I can take tests easily. Like Gladys, I wish we still used IQ tests so I could know my mental capacity better than I do now. It is good to know how to take tests well, as they are used widely in education. The Gladys Dart School prepares us well.

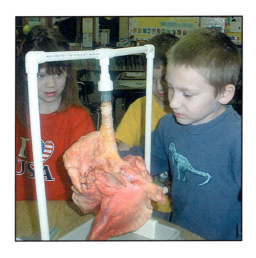

Chapter 13
Technology

CHAPTER **13**

Technology

When we first reestablished the school in Manley Hot Springs in 1958, kerosene Coleman lanterns lighted it. We had an outdated globe and a battery operated radio. That was the extent of our audio/visual equipment. When I retired in 1987, high technology had entered the classroom and we utilized its benefits to every extent within our means. Technology was breaking down the educational walls and opening the classroom to the world.

When we purchased our own generator in 1959 to supply electricity to our school, it opened a wide door to technology that depended on electric power. Now books competed with equipment that operated records, filmstrips, and movies. For me books still occupied the favorite place on the library shelf.

The computer, however, was the revolutionary tool education could exploit with limitless opportunity. We were fortunate to have computers introduced into our village schools in the early 70's, thanks to a visionary superintendent, Joe Cooper, who saw their potential from the start.

At the time I was the principal-teacher in Manley Hot Springs. It was still a one-room school. That meant I had the primary responsibility for the education of a multi-grade enrolment, which was between a dozen and two-dozen students at that time. I also was the administrator of the school so I was responsible for the maintenance of the school and the staff. I was also the liaison through the Community School Committee between the school and the community. I was also the liaison between the school through the administration with the regional school board. This was occurring in a time of rapid change in technology and all the complications that come with such a change. It meant that you had all of this responsibility with the primary focus teaching what was best and right for each student.

Meeting these responsibilities meant averaging ten to twelve hours a day during the week and more weekends than not. I had no clue where I could find the time and energy to institute a computer program with that kind of schedule

Miracles happen. At this very time a newcomer to our town, Liza Vernet, came to school to ask me if there was a chance she could do some volunteer work. I spoke of my dilemma and desperate need because I knew the computer program would be a full time responsibility. To my students and my good fortune and eternal gratitude, she accepted the challenge.

I do not know how Liza accomplished what she did. We were given the computers with only a negligible amount of instruction or help and next to no hardware and software equipment. I remember her first classes with the students were to disassemble the computers to familiarize the students with the equipment. She also set strict standards of care and behavior when they were using the computer.   Slowly, some software began to arrive. Things improved rapidly. All of the students were involved in the computer program. One-day a teacher's aide, Cindy Pearson, came to me and told me their computer skills would be improved if they could use the keyboard more efficiently. When I told her we could not expect our youngest children's little fingers to reach the keys like typists do, she replied, "We teach them piano, don't we?"

I was grateful someone recognized the situation and was ready to challenge my opinion as a teacher because the students were the greatest beneficiaries as a result. It harked back to my childhood again. When we were challenged or disagreed on a subject and could not get beyond the "yes, it is" and "no, it isn't" stage, my father would stop us and tell us to go and get facts to back up our position. Then he would make us come back, state our case, and said, "Let the best man win." I have had students, even first graders, who felt free to challenge me and win me over. It just proves you are never too old to learn and never too young to teach.

So my teacher-aide brought her typing text to school. All the students learned the keyboard. The speed at which their keyboarding skills improved was in direct ratio to the speed they were learning computer programs.

In those early days, I attended a state teacher's conference and there were several companies representing computers. I spent time at each exhibit because I wanted to bring back to the classroom any help I could find. I remember asking one expert at what age they recommended children should start computer training. He said the middle elementary level would be the earliest time to introduce the computer. I told him we started ours at the kindergarten level. I do not think he believed me, because he quickly turned and started talking to another person. I presumed our conversation was over.

We had an itinerant vocational education coordinator who told us he had nothing to offer in the vocational education area on computers. Liza offered and created her own program. The course involved three students. They formed a business in computer graphics. They sold signs and banners. They elected officers and the business was required to keep financial and activity records. The success of their program was rewarded by an invitation to demonstrate their project at a statewide teacher's conference.

When software became more available, and it did at a rapid pace, I was able to work with Liza to help our students. I studied the results of students' performances mostly from standardized test results, but from other sources as well. They would reveal areas where students would benefit from remedial, supplemental, or enrichment material. Liza would find software that would serve our needs. The programs produced some exciting results. It is another example of the "preview-review" aspect of teaching that is uniquely possible in a one-room school and the diversity it naturally offers.

When I see what is happening with the capabilities of the computer in the classroom today, what we started with seems like ancient history. When we instituted the computer program it was in a room that was nothing more than a large closet. It was a room that had shelves of teacher's editions and materials, a piano for our music program, and one computer.

When the school building was enlarged, we designed a computer room next to the library, and all the computer activity was contained in that room. Now computers are used inside and outside the school. It is symbolic of what education is all about. Computers have made the world—indeed, the cosmos and beyond—an open classroom.

When I had my last science lesson before my retirement with my upper elementary students, we were discussing a science newsletter that included an article on the Hubble Telescope. I told them I was going to miss the excitement in the classroom sharing the wonders that Hubble would bring as it explored the newest frontier. I wandered off the subject by also telling them how fortunate we were just being here to witness these events. Our own presence was a miracle created by love. The Hubble was a miracle created by the power of an educated mind.

Technology is only a tool. How we learn to use it and what we do with it tells us what kind of persons we are.

Alfred's Words

Since the Gladys Dart School is so small, computers are a necessity in the learning process. We could not learn so much without the Internet, nor write so much without a keyboard. The students here use multiple portable hard-drives, take online classes, and edit all of our writing with the computers. Technology is definitely a major component of this school.

Mrs. Wright and Mrs. Redington at Graduation Night

Part 3
In Deed, Indeed

Upon the subject of education, not presuming to dictate any plan or system respecting it, I can only say that I view it as the most important subject which we as a people can be engaged in.

> Abraham Lincoln
> March 9, 1832
> First Political Announcement

Chapter 14
Tolerance

CHAPTER **14**

Tolerance

When I have been asked how I wanted to be remembered as a teacher, I always gave the same answer. I wanted to be remembered for my daily performance in the classroom. When I have been asked what value I rated the highest, I did not have an answer. I was able to say that I thought tolerance rated as high as any because it reflected every attitude and action as a teacher and a person.

Tolerance is such a strong driving force in our lives, yet its wisdom is difficult to find in a book of instruction we can use to teach us how we should act. It is because actions speak louder than words, I guess. Tolerance is best taught and learned by example for that reason. This is what I have learned about tolerance.

"Remember, Gladdie," (that is what my father always called me) "you're no better than anyone else--but you're just as good." I can recall my father telling me that when I was six years old because I was in the first grade at the time. I also recall it was in a casual conversation, but I do not remember in what context it was spoken. It became my definition of tolerance.

One example of intolerance was an account my father related of an incident that occurred shortly after his arrival in Minnesota. My father was a man of great strength and stamina and he found his first job in a logging camp. For whatever reason, a group of his coworkers began to ridicule him for his inadequate English and Finnish accent. One day the taunts sounded louder and became more serious. A Native American Indian, who was even bigger and stronger than my father, who came to work every day and rarely said a word to anybody, went to my father's side and in a loud voice told the others if anybody gave my father any more static he would be at my father's side to help him. There were no more incidents, and a lasting friendship was the result.

Intolerance is based mostly on ignorance. The need to understand

IN DEED INDEED

differences in any form is an objective we recognize as teachers. Although the roots and events of intolerance sometimes can be historically documented and taught, the remedy is more difficult to find.

The lessons in tolerance for me were best set by examples I vividly remember. This is an account of such an example. It happened in the days of the Great Depression.

The train went through the center of our small town, and when we heard the whistle, which would be about a mile away, we would run to a spot where we would watch it go by. It became such a common practice that we got to recognize the engineers, the conductors, and the brakemen, who would toot the whistle and wave to us as they went by. When the freight trains went by, we would count the boxcars and the oil tankers.

During the Depression, people would ride in the boxcars and we would count them. They were mainly in the trains going west. They were people who had lost everything during the Depression and they were going out west where the promise of a new life seemed more attainable and attractive. I remember being startled one day when I was counting the people and I saw a boxcar with the big doors wide open. Inside there was a family of four, parents and two small children. The mother was on her knees washing clothes in a small pail. The impact of that scene seemed to turn a few seconds into an eternity.

We called these travelers hobos. Some people called them bums, but we always called them hobos. Sometimes when the trains slowed down or stopped altogether to switch some cars to or from a third track, the hobos would get off. The hobos that did get off always got off for the same reason. They were hungry. Since we owned the only store in town, they usually went there first. Most of them did not have enough money to buy food.

Those that did not never begged for food. They would ask my father if anyone had work so they could buy some food. My father never gave them food from the store. He would direct them to our home. He said my mother would give them something to eat and, in the meantime, he would find some job they could do in payment.

Mother's offering was always the same. A loaf or loaves of bread, some butter, something to drink, and whatever she had on hand to make sandwiches.

Since my father was depot custodian, he would let them stay there at night if they needed to get out of the weather. It was usually only for one night, since freight trains came on a daily schedule most of the time. There was a coal stove he gave them permission to use to keep them dry and warm.

Our parents and the parents of our friends encouraged us children to visit the hobos in the depot in the evening when our chores were done. We were

TOLERANCE

told they were all good people who had run into some bad luck and they were looking for a better life.

We really enjoyed and looked forward to these visits because each one was different, entertaining, and educationally revealing. Our pattern was the same. We always spent the evening with one of us saying, "We will all sing you a song if you tell us a story about you."

We would sing our hearts out because we knew we would be rewarded with entertaining stories they would tell and we were anxious to hear. And then they were gone, either during the night or the next day when the train rolled westward. They are faded memories, but the lesson in tolerance is not.

In three instances my memory is very clear. The first one is a young man with his son who was "riding the rails" and got off in our town because they had nothing to eat. He told my father he was a sign painter. After my mother had supplied him with food for the day my father asked him if he could paint a sign that could be put over the door to the store. My father gave him the materials and freedom to name it, design it, and paint it. It took him two days. We had a large sign "Reed's Store" in red letters on a white background.

During my visit home before I left for Alaska I noticed it was faded and chipped, so I repainted it. Years later my mother sold all her property after my father's death. She donated the store to the community to be used as a community hall. The community did some interior remodeling, painted the building white, and renamed the building "The Little White House."

Many years later when I made my first trip back to Minnesota from Alaska, I asked if I might have the sign if no one else had taken it, but it was too late. I was told it was burned as scrap when it became community property. I also remember the sign painter because it was one of two times, as far as I know, that my father gave money to a hobo. The price of the sign was three nights in the depot, food my mother gave them during that period, and a couple of one dollar bills my father put in the painter's hand when he said goodbye.

Our favorite hobo was the only one I remember by name. His name was Max Young. He was also the only one that returned after his first visit. He came back five times, and it was usually in the fall.

We would visit him each night in the depot and he loved to hear us sing. He would say, "I'll tell you a story of this past year if you sing me three songs."

There were two songs he always requested. One was "Silver Haired Daddy of Mine" and the other was a hobo song our mother taught us. We were taught the chorus and one verse, although I've been told there were more.

IN DEED INDEED

The words to the hobo song are:
Chorus
Hallelujah, I'm a bum
Hallelujah, bum again
Hallelujah, give us a handout
To revive us again

Verse
I went to the door
And I asked for some bread
The lady said, "Scram, bum
The baker is dead"

My mother, when she taught us the song, insisted we could only sing it changing the third line in the verse to say, "The lady said, Bum, Bum." She also changed the last line to say, "I'll give you some bread." My mother's revision carries its own message on tolerance. Hobo songs are favorites of mine to this day.

One fall day in 1937 we were coming home on the school bus. We were about a half-dozen miles from home when we saw a man walking homeward. We recognized him as Max Young. We yelled to the bus driver to stop because he was our friend coming to visit us. The bus driver stopped and Max went home with us.

He went to see my father at the store. When he was settled in at the depot and my mother had sent him food, we had our usual visit that evening.

My father had noticed a change in Max's stamina and appearance, and convinced him to see our family doctor, where my father took him. It was confirmed that Max had tuberculosis. My father offered his help. Because Max had a half African American and half Native American birthright, my father was able to get him admitted to a tuberculosis sanitarium. He took him there and visited him a few times before he died within the year. We were told of Max's illness after his death.

The third instance were two young men none of us met except my father. The two men did not come by train like most hobos did. They had walked and hitch-hiked from town to town from somewhere in the east up to the Iron Range in northern Minnesota to our place on their way westward, like so many others had before them.

My father recognized that they looked so desperate he did not even direct them to my mother first. Instead, from the store, he gave them a loaf of bread, two rings of bologna, butter, and milk to drink. They found a spot on a bank opposite the store, which was located on the main highway. My father observed them as they finished all the food with relish.

Then he engaged them in conversation. They told him they wanted to keep moving. My father suggested he thought he could get them a ride to the next town shortly, and he went to verify it. He gave them another round of food and two dollars to take with them after the man picked them up. That night at the dinner table he told us what had happened.

The story did not end there. More than two decades later, my father was on one of his trips out West at the invitation of his church. His doctor at home told him he could make the trip only if he consulted with doctors on his trip. He had just had surgery for skin cancer that resulted from his smoking, and they wanted him to keep a close check on it.

He also took time on this trip to visit a daughter who lived in Seattle. While there, he went to see a doctor as he had promised he would do. When he got back to my sister's home, she asked him how his trip was.

He said it was a very interesting one. The doctor had come in to check him out. When he saw my father's name on the chart, he asked him if he was from Automba, Minnesota. When my father said he was, the doctor introduced himself as one of the men who had sat on a bank opposite the store and ate what he called the best meal of his life. After the consultation my father asked him how much he owed him. The doctor replied, "How can I charge you anything after you saved the day and maybe my life that day?"

This is the essence of tolerance. We are our brothers' and sisters' keeper and we do it because it is the right thing to do.

I do not use these memories to lecture anybody. I do use these memories to guide me in my behavior. Although words are great, actions speak louder.

Alfred's Words

Tolerance is my favorite chapter of Gladys's book. I really loved this chapter because of all the positive messages it carries to those who read it. After telling me about the song "Hallelujah, I'm a bum" Gladys and I had a conversation about the tolerance chapter where she told me of a man who had explained to her that there were many more verses to the song. I was so interested that I looked up the song online and found there were more than 10 other verses. After seeing these and taking them to Gladys I found out why her mother had never told Gladys or her other children the additional verses. The song talked mainly about drinking and gambling, whereas Gladys's mother would not let a deck of cards or a drink of alcohol into her house.

Tolerance is taught daily in the Gladys Dart School. Because of the tolerance level in the school, there are never major arguments in the school. This could be due to the low student to teacher ratio, but I like to think that we are tolerant. We are taught here to accept all races, cultures, and religious peoples. In this small school there is no chance to exclude others.

Romeo & Juliet Go to America on the Titanic—Dinner Theatre Play

Chapter 15
The Last Word

CHAPTER **15**

The Last Word

Politics and religion are areas where teachers have to be sensitive to balance restrictions and responsibility but they are part of who we are, so I thought it should be addressed.

I did not think I crossed the line when I talked about politics in terms of a civic duty. I did not think I crossed the line when we had mock campaigns during elections. Students would choose which candidate they wanted to portray. It was their job to research the facts independently and debate the issues with great freedom. Finally, they would have to convince the electorate, their classmates, and a mock election would decide the winner. They also campaigned in the same manner when student elections of any kind were deemed necessary.

I was a neutral observer with no vote. Living in a small community and knowing the families well, I noticed that children were mainly influenced by their parent's politics.

However, that did not mean they did not ask me about my politics. With honesty, I would state my beliefs, but I would not promote or defend them. Manley Hot Springs is a small town that historically has been mainly conservative Republican. My husband and I were part of a small minority that were active liberal Democrats. My own family consisted of Democrats, Republicans, Independents, or no party affiliation. We enjoyed lively political discussions, but it was not at the expense of our respect for each other or our views.

The only exception I remember goes back to the Great Depression when we were suffering economically with no end in sight. Some people thought Communism offered promise and hope. I remember my parent's opposition to the philosophy of Communism. It was the first time they expressed a position in adamant, unwavering terms. They did not leave any opening for debate.

I was reminded of this more than fifty years later when my sister, who was a linguist at the University of Alaska, told me this incident. My mother was living with her after we lost our father. She had sold her property and eventually came to Alaska.

My sister Irene had been working with some Russian linguists at the University. She would invite them to her home and my mother, who helped her feed and entertain them, got to know them quite well. It was also during this same period my mother was diagnosed with a recurrence of cancer, and my sister flew with her to Seattle for medical attention.

While they were in flight, my sister asked my mother if she was feeling all right. My mother laughed as she replied, "Oh yes, I feel fine, but I think we left just in time. I was beginning to love those Communists."

In my family we have Protestants, Catholics, Jehovah's Witnesses, others with some Jewish background, and still others who do not belong to any organized church.

In school years we celebrated Christmas and recognized Hanukah as a history lesson rather than a lesson in faith. Unfortunately, we unintentionally overlooked other faiths. I was reminded of this when I taught in a large school in Fairbanks and I had students who were Jehovah's Witnesses. When we had holidays or occasions they did not celebrate, I contacted the parents and, with earlier approval from the principal, I asked them if they wanted to organize an activity in the library or some other neutral area while we partied. I told them they should invite other students of the same faith who were attending school to join them during that period. It seemed to work out well.

It happened rarely, but whenever my students asked me what my politics or religion were, I believed they deserved an honest answer. I would tell them, but I would never elaborate the reasons for my choice because I wanted to avoid discussion on the subject while we were in school.

I would tell them I was a liberal Democrat. I also told them the Dalai Lama expressed my spiritual faith better than I could when he said:

This is my simple religion
There is no need for temples
No need for complicated philosophy
Our own brain, our own heart is our temple
The philosophy is kindness.

However, there was one area that was an unusually strong expression of my spirituality, deeply rooted in my Finnish heritage. It was a reverence of the individual spirit from birth to beyond the grave.

Cemeteries were hallowed grounds and our departed ones were cared for with love and respect. When a relative from Finland visited us for the first time we went to pick him up at the airport sixty miles away. At his request, we stopped at the cemetery on our way home.

When my sister Irene, daughter Diane, and future daughter-in-law Liza and I visited relatives in Finland some years later, a visit to the cemetery was placed on their agenda of places to go. While we were at the cemetery, I was curious about a meticulously kept area that was adjacent to the cemetery. We were told they were Russians buried there. They had died in the Russo-Finnish War of '39-'40. The Russians had not been claimed by their families or the government. Others were granted burial by special request from their survivors.

We were told there was a Finnish custom that included a visit to the cemetery to pay their respects to the departed that was part of many wedding celebrations. There also is a Christmas Eve ritual we still practice in our family where we will bring candles to the family gravesite and sing "Silent Night."

I go to the cemetery throughout the year most frequently from spring through fall. While some might call it unusual or morbid it gives me an added spiritual sense of comfort and peace.

There was one occasion in the classroom when I was confronted about the subject of the spirit. It was the last period in the day and we had just completed a health class with the upper elementary students.

I had dismissed the students for the day. One of the students, Mark Evans, waited until he thought everyone had gone. He came up to me and asked, "Why do you just teach us all about the body and we never learn anything about our spirit?"

When I told him, as a teacher, I followed the guidelines in our curriculum and teaching the spirit wasn't part of it, he replied, "Well, can you pretend you're not my teacher so we can talk about it?"

I told him, "On that condition, of course I will. Just give me time to think about it. In fact, I will make it my homework assignment and I will report to you when I have completed it."

It was then that we noticed another student, David Lee, had been listening to us. They walked out together.

I could not get the conversation out of my mind. I knew the answer I wanted was in some book or article I had read. Favorite pastime reading for me was on the topics of humanism and spiritualism.

I went to bed that night with an unfinished homework assignment. Sometime during the night I experienced a revelation I had had on two other separate occasions. I can liken it to finding the final pieces to a difficult puzzle. The pieces were there, and it was a matter of putting them all together. When morning came, I had found the pieces that gave me the answer.

After I had dismissed the students the next day, both Mark and David stayed behind. I knew then that they must have talked about it with each other the day before.

Mark asked me if I had done my homework. I told him someone had done it for me, but I could not remember the name or the exact words used, or in which book I could find it.

So, I paraphrased the answer, "I believe the soul is the very essence that embodies our being. I further believe it is the spirit that expresses the beauty of our soul." I asked Mark if that satisfied him in the search of his spirit. He said it did, but he still wanted me to tell him where I had read it when I found the answer. I asked him to look for it as well. Then we would share what either of us found.

It was then that David said, "But beauty is in the eyes of the beholder. Isn't that what they say?"

That did not require another homework assignment. I spontaneously responded, "Yes, and I believe that's what makes us unique individuals."

I will always be grateful for the conversation we had. We were never able to finalize our conversation because Mark and David, with eleven other students I had taught in Manley Hot Springs, have gone to their final resting place in our local cemetery.

As for me, I am still searching.

THE LAST WORD

FIFTY YEARS!